DARK SHADES

and

LEMONADE

fresh
light-hearted
enhancements
for long term
relationships

Glenda L Witherspoon M.Ed.

ISBN: 1456577581
ISBN-13: 9781456577582

To "my cowboy" and husband, Hank for providing the loving environment for me to explore and to my "ultimates", Erica Dione, Tasha Jhene Lois, Tamara Leigh, Krista Mone' and Lance Edward; you are the best!

Dark shades and lemonade...cultivating an environment for loving, long-term relationships.

We are living longer than ever before; thus, relationships are extending. What do we do when "together forever" has exceeded the years we expected or even imagined?

What path should we take? Call it quits, remain in an unfulfilling relationship, or create a journey of discovering the good of long-term togetherness? I choose the latter.

Title Background

Sitting in outdoor concerts sometime ago, I noticed all the people wearing dark shades and I began to think about the reason we wear sunglasses. Protection from the sunrays is the primary benefit, but the benefit of camouflaging one's eye- focus is definitely another benefit. This serves us well in our freedom to look at someone or something without being detected.

Drinking lemonade, as I was at the time, served to prevent the uttering of words or exclamations that will reveal our focus and thoughts.

I surmised that dark shades and lemonade would assist in maintaining our relationships. Thusly, Dark Shades and Lemonade became the title of this book. Enjoy!

This book was written to provide quick and to the point thoughts to consider in building and maintaining positive relationships. It is intended to be used as a working tool to keep with you to refer to and put into action on a regular basis.

My hope is that you will find the thoughts to ponder and space to note your comments and reflect-ions a convenient source of support in your quest for a loving relationship.

"Shades and Lemonade"

Dark shades allows us to look at something or someone and our observation is not detected.

Dark shades give our loved one the sense that they are our focus and not something or someone else.

 ∽

Dark shades allow you to navigate life without the glaring light of others reading your eyes to find something other than your stated words. Dark shades prevent others from reading anything into your conversation.

Dark shades shield from others misreading your focus.

Dark shades decrease the glaring light of scrutiny.

Dark shades camouflage.

Dark shades protect.

Dark shades provide privacy.

Dark shades camouflage.

Dark shades protect.

Dark shades provide privacy.

Dark shades prevent your partner from reading into your statements, and maintains the happy and peaceful relationship environment.

Drinking lemonade occupies your mouth allowing you to think of positive words to say and refreshes you, maintains the loveliness in your voice, provides a grace period to think about the benefits of partner's choice.

Lemonade pushes out all of the toxins that are generated throughout the relationship.

Drinking lemonade sweetens all situations and occupies your mouth to prevent verbalizing venomous thoughts, while you formulate kind words to minimize negative outcome.

∽

"Other Thoughts"

Contemplation of the happy relationship and not the demise of the relationship is what creates and moves all efforts toward the goal of lasting love.

Instead of considering what issues will prompt you to end the relationship, plan for and concentrate on proactive actions to build a lasting partnership, for it is the contemplation of a thing that renders that thing.

The choosing of one's attitude toward the challenge is the most important element that determines the outcome.

Learning to navigate life by choosing to be happy no matter the situation shines a good light all issues and persons. Enter your environment from a different door, a different mindset.

You can spend a lifetime in misery and suspicious-ness, or operate in positive thoughts.

Know that what you need to know will find its way to you.

Listen to the whisper thoughts.

Resist becoming the goddess/god of correction of others.

Plan to forgive before asked and prepare to meet challenges with kindness.

Don't allow others to change your happy persona.

Find the good. Look for the positives. Uncover the good in each situation.

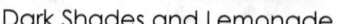

Cultivate the eagerness of young love.

Provide an environment that replenishes the innocent trusting heart.

Plan to increase the love when impending contention begins to seep in.

Enjoy the right now, not the next time, or the past.

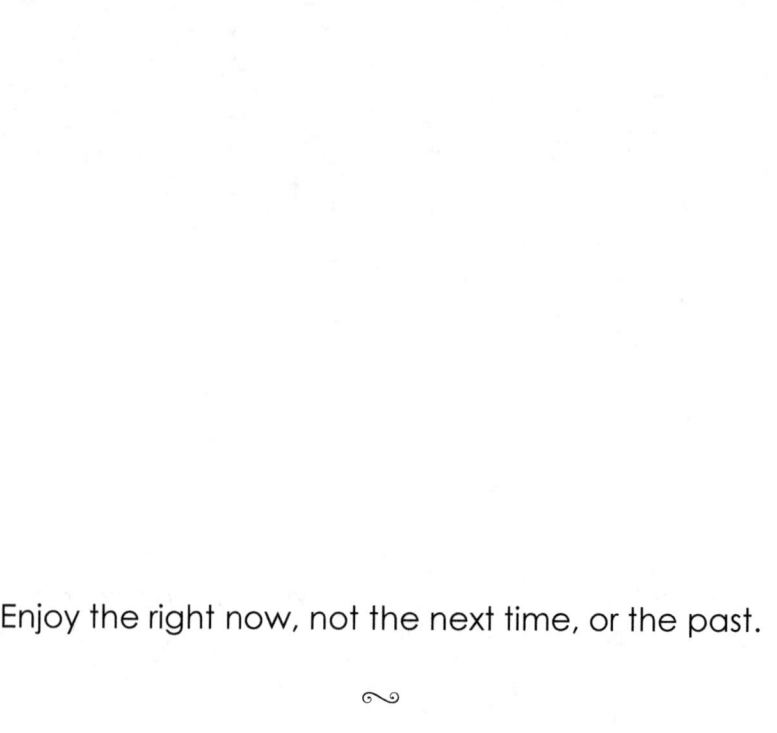

Press down unfounded suspicion with youthful trust.

Don't allow others into the scope of your dark shades.

Contemplate happiness and plan happiness, and then you will discover the pathways that lead to perpetual happiness.

∽

Evaluate all relationship issues through the lens of your dark shades. Keeps focus on important matters.

Fresh love engenders trust, so freshen it regularly by entertaining thoughts of the happiness you share.

Continue the chase—catch me if you can. Maintain the individual that attracted him/her to you.

Create mystery by not allowing free, constant access to your rawness (your essence, and the not-so-lovely you).

Always be the girlfriend. Surprise your partner with your sexiness. Surprise through the continuing evolution of you.

Always bettering never settling.

∽

The push-pull effect engenders a contemplation of the value of you to the other.

"Jerk the chain" to shake up the mundane.

Predictability is the foundation of boredom.

Listen more than you talk.

Refrain from the statement, "I need to talk." Eventually the talk will happen. Talk when opportunity presents.

Listen with your heart of love without prejudice of past events and issues.

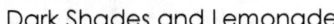

Give ultimate care to the relationship. Always give time to contemplate the growing of a happy relationship.

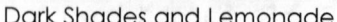

The amount of time and effort that go into seeking the things to create an environment in which love can thrive is directly related to the condition of the relationship.

Time and care for the relationship are not the same as housekeeping, childcare, and other required duties.

The care and nurturing of love is essential to the longevity of the relationship.

Impromptu acts of "I just needed to be with you, hear your voice, feel your touch" excite and tantalize the mind and body.

∾

Interject yourself into the world of your relationship partner.

Seeing the reaction of others toward you gives your partner an appreciation of you from a larger perspective.

Choose to be happy. It is your decision.

Your happiness must not be determined by others, and/or the challenges you face.

Happy must become part of your persona.

Focus your heart outward instead of inward on self. A heart that focuses outward is not consumed with self.

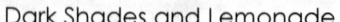

Maintain the "it" that brought you together.

Remember FUN is important; make it a top priority.

∽

Remember the good actions and interactions that work well. Make a note of then in this book. Refer to your notes regularly to remind yourself.

∽

Plan for lasting love.

Young love happen continued love must be nurtured and cultivated.

༄

Coupleship is best served by eliminating the expectation that all free time should be spent together.

Maintain control of your heart.

You decide your emotions; never release control of how you live to anyone.

You were chosen...ACT LIKE IT!

∽

Self-sufficiency (independence) is not a part of a coupleship. Interdependency is key to a lasting relationship.

Independence and self-sufficiency vs. interdependence and self-efficiency—know the difference.

∽

Let go of self-guilt.

Someone cares for you the way you are. Imperfections make you unique.

Enjoy the right now; don't contemplate the "what ifs" of life.

Rid the relationship of the little sand issues that are irritants in the relationship's gears.

Ignore all the distractions; put focus on your goals of happiness and you will have happiness.

RELATIONSHIP LONGEVITY ACTIVITY

Rate each of the statements according to your behavior.

1 do not agree

2 somewhat agree

3 totally agree

1. I accept my partner's need to have outside interests that don't include me.

2. I cultivate my own passions and interests.

3. I listen to others' opinion about my partner's shortcomings.

4. I listen and make efforts to understand my partner's point of view.

5. Commitment to always look for the good in all challenges and issues is a top priority for me.

6. 6 Angry confrontation is always a part of relationships.

7. Without trust, the partnership is doomed.

8. I must always get my point across.

9. Being happy is a choice.

10. I think that my partner's leisure time should be spent with me.

A score of 1-9 indicates you should incorporate more of the books thoughts into your interactions with your partner.

A score of 10-20 indicates you have good relationship longevity potential.

A score of 21-30 indicates great relationship longevity potential.

"May we all have a wonderful collection of dark shades and an endless supply of refreshing lemonade." ~ Glenda

Notes and Memories

Notes and Memories

Notes and Memories

Notes and Memories

www.ingramcontent.com/pod-product-compliance
Lightning Source LLC
Chambersburg PA
CBHW062116280526
45788CB00003B/1486